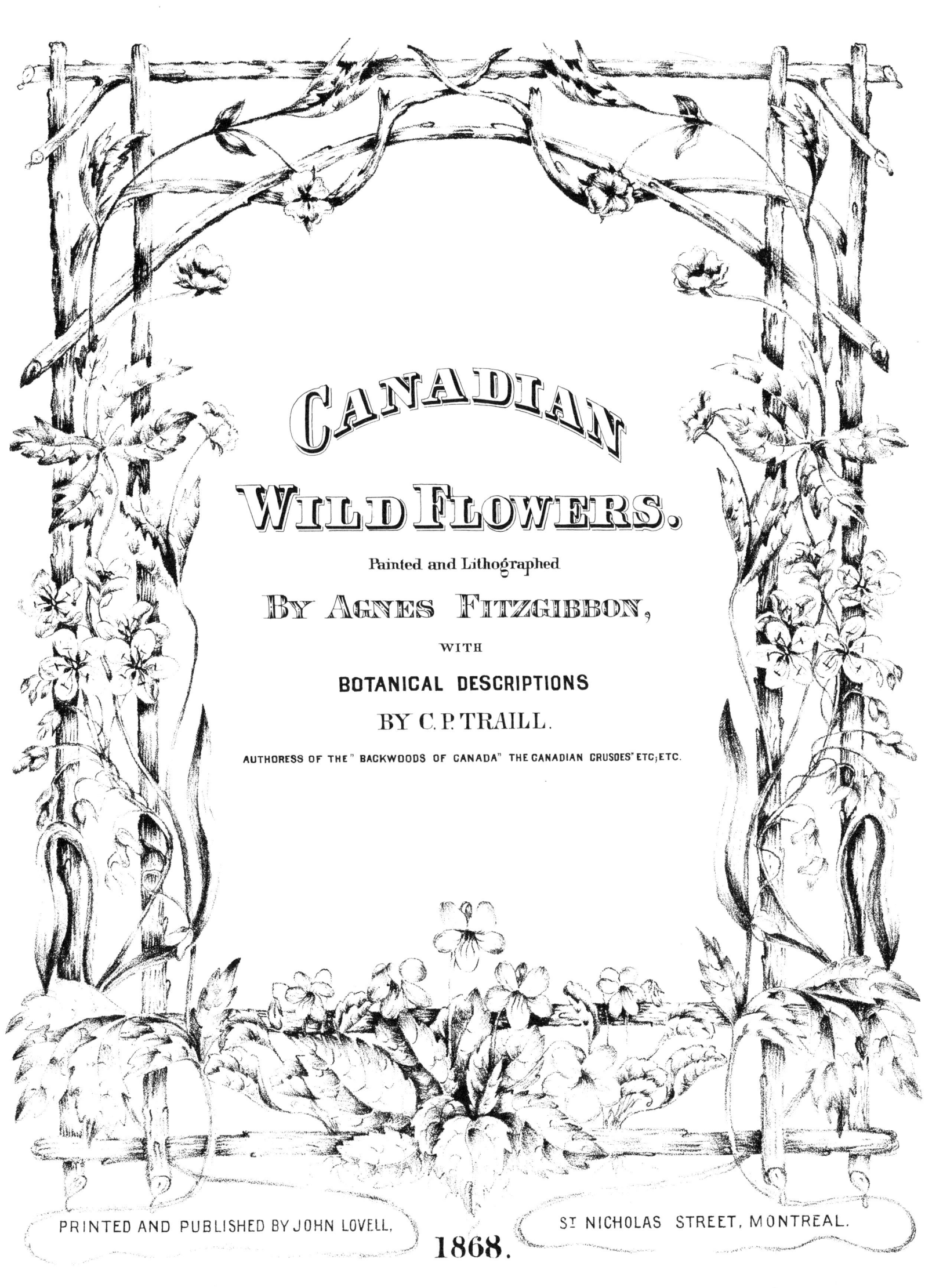

Canadian Wild Flowers.

Painted and Lithographed

By Agnes Fitzgibbon,

with

Botanical Descriptions

By C. P. Traill.

AUTHORESS OF THE "BACKWOODS OF CANADA" THE CANADIAN CRUSOES" ETC; ETC.

PRINTED AND PUBLISHED BY JOHN LOVELL, ST NICHOLAS STREET, MONTREAL.

1868.

COLES CANADIANA COLLECTION

Originally published in 1868
by John Lovell
St. Nicholas Street, Montreal

Facsimile edition published
by COLES PUBLISHING COMPANY, Toronto
Printed in Canada
© Copyright 1972.

CONTENTS.

PLATE I. .... *facing page 8*

                                                            TEXT ON PAGE.

Indian Turnip.—*Arum triphyllum (Arum family)* 9
Showy Orchis.—*Orchis Spectabilis* 13
Painted Cup, Scarlet Cup.—*Castillèia Coccínea* 15
Cone Flower.—*Rudbéckia fulgida* 19

PLATE II. .... *facing page 16*   TEXT ON PAGE.

Sweet Wintergreen.—*Pyrola ellíptica* 21
One Flowered Pyrola.—*Monèses uniflorà* 24
Flowering Raspberry.—*Rùbus Odorátus* 25
Speedwell.—American Brooklime.—*Veronica Americàna* 27

PLATE III. .... *facing page 24*   TEXT ON PAGE.

Adders-Tongue.—Dog-Toothed Violet.—*Erythrònium Americánum* 29
White Trillium.—Death-Flower.—*Tríllium Grandiflòrum* 31
Rock Columbine.—*Aquilègia Canadénsis* 34

PLATE IV. .... *facing page 32*   TEXT ON PAGE.

Squirrel Corn.—*Dicéntra Canadénsis* 37
Purple Trillium.—Death-Flower.—Birth-Root.—*Tríllium eréctum* 39
Wood Gerànium.—Cranes-Bill.—*Gerànium maculàtum* 41
Chickweed Wintergreen.—*Trientàlis* 44

cont'd over

CONTENTS.

PLATE V.............................*facing page 40*

TEXT ON PAGE.

Yellow Lady's Slippers.—*Cypripèdium parviflòrum and Cypripèdium pubéscens*..... 45
Large Blue Flag.—*Iris Versicolor.—Fleur-de-luce*... 47
Small Cranberry.—*Vaccínium Oxycóccus*.. 50

PLATE VI.............................*facing page 48*

TEXT ON PAGE.

Wild Orange Lily.—*Lílium Philadélphicum*... 53
Canadian Harebell.—*Campánula Rotundifólia*.. 56
Showy Lady's Slipper.—*Cypripèdium Spectàbile*.—(Moccasin Flower)............ 59

PLATE VII.............................*facing page 56*

TEXT ON PAGE.

Early Wild Rose.—*Ròsa Blánda*... 63
Pentstèmon Beard-Tongue.—*Pentstèmon pubéscens*... 66

PLATE VIII.............................*facing page 64*

TEXT ON PAGE.

Sweet Scented Water Lily.—*Nymphæa Odoràta*... 67
Yellow Pond Lily.—*Nùphar Ádvena*.—(Spatter Dock.)....................................... 71

PLATE IX.............................*facing page 72*

TEXT ON PAGE.

Pitcher Plant.—(Soldier's Drinking Cup.)—*Sarracènia Purpùrea*...................... 73

PLATE X.............................*facing page 80*

TEXT ON PAGE.

Liver-Leaf—Wind-Flower.—(Sharp Lobed Hepática.)—*Hepàtica Acutíloba*.......... 77
Bellwort.—(Wood Daffodil.)—*Uvulària Grandiflòra*.. 79
Wood Anemòne.—*Anemòne Nemoròsa*... 81
Spring Beauty.—*Claytònia Virgínica*.. 84

PREFACE.

A FEW words of introduction for our book on the Wild Flowers of Canada may be deemed necessary by the friends who have so kindly and freely come forward as Subscribers to the work, and also the public in general.

We present it with every hope that success may follow the publication, which has been delayed, by many unforeseen obstacles, from appearing at as early a date as had been anticipated. However, we must fall back upon the old saying—'Better late than never'—and in excuse, observe that the labour of the undertaking has been very great. First, the designs—all the flowers having been copied from NATURE'S OWN BOOK, by MRS. FITZGIBBON—then the subsequent grouping and lithographing on stone *by her own hand*, and finally the colouring of each separate plate—a gigantic effort to be executed by one person.

With a patriotic pride in her native land, Mrs. F. was desirous that the book should be entirely of Canadian production, without any foreign aid, and thus far her design has been carried out; whether successfully or not, remains for the public to decide.

Any short-comings that may be noticed by our friends, must be excused on the score of the work being wholly Canadian in its execution.

Our Canadian Publishers can hardly be expected to compete with the booksellers and printers of the Old Country, or of the United States, labouring as they must necessarily do in a new country under many mechanical disadvantages.

Thus far, then, in behalf of the artist and publisher—a few words remain yet to be said as regards the literary portion of the book.

Many years ago the only work that treated in any way of the Wild Plants of Canada, the country owed to that indefatigable botanist, Frederick Pursh, whose valuable labours were but little appreciated in the country in which he toiled and died—it is to be feared but poorly rewarded during his life.

The land, with all its rich vegetable resources, lay as it were an untrodden wilderness for many years, save by those hardy settlers who cared little for the forest flowers that grew in their paths.

The unlettered *Indians*, indeed, culled a few of the herbs and barks and roots for healing purposes, and dyes wherewith to stain their squaws' basket-work and porcupine quills; and some of the old settlers had given them local and descriptive names by which they may be recognized even in the present day, but there was no one to give written descriptions, or to compile a native Flora, or even domestic Herbal of the Wild Plants of Canada. The subject seemed to excite little interest, unless in some chance traveller whom curiosity or business brought to the country. But now the schoolmaster is abroad, and better things are, we trust, in store for this our noble country.

Much valuable and interesting matter has already been given to the world, and many works still in progress are, we hear, likely to be added to our scientific literature.

It was to supply a deficiency that has long been felt in this country, that the Authoress first conceived the idea of writing a little volume descriptive of the most remarkable of the Wild Flowers, Shrubs and Forest Trees of Canada.

This work, *seen in MS.*, received the sanction and approval of several scientific and literary gentlemen in Canada, among whom were Dr. Hincks and Prof. George Lawson; but want of funds on the part of the writer, prevented the publication of the work. And finally it was at last agreed that the Book of Canadian Wild Flowers should be the work of Mrs. FitzGibbon, and the descriptions of the plants as delineated by her hand, should be selected and adapted to suit the subjects of the Plates from Mrs. Traill's MS.

The scientific reader may possibly expect a more learned description of the Plants, and may notice many defects and omissions; while others who are indifferent to the subject, may on the other hand think that there are too many botanical terms introduced. It is difficult to please two parties. We crave indulgence for all errors, promising that in another volume, should our present book be kindly received, we will endeavour to render it as perfect as our limited knowledge will allow us to do. And so we bid our readers heartily farewell, wishing them much pleasure and contentment, and that its contents, both artistical and literary, may serve to foster a love for the native plants of Canada, and turn their attention to the floral beauty that is destined sooner or later to be swept away, as the onward march of civilization clears away the primeval forest—reclaims the swamps and bogs, and turns the waste places into a fruitful field. The lover of flowers may then look in vain for our sweet-scented Pyrolas and Slipper-plants, and be forced to say in the words of the old Scottish song—

" The flowers of the forest are a' wede away."

O wail for the forest, the proud stately forest,
No more its dark depths shall the hunter explore,
For the bright golden grain,
Shall wave free o'er the plain,
O wail for the forest, its glories are o'er.

C. P. TRAILL.

TORONTO, December, 1868.

1. CASTILLEIA COCCINEA. (Scarlet painted Cup.)   2. ORCHIS SPECTABILIS (Showy Orchis.)   3. ARUM TRIPHYLLUM. (Indian Turnip.)   4. RUDBECKIA FULGIDA. (Cone Flower.)

Indian Turnip.

Arum triphyllum (Arum family.)

"Or peers the Arum from its spotted veil."
                                    BRYANT.

THERE are two species of Arums common to Canada, the larger of which is known as Green-dragon (Arum Dracontium); the other, which forms the central figure in the plate, is the most common to our soil, and is known by the familiar name of INDIAN TURNIP (*Arum triphyllum* or *A. purpureum*).

These moisture-loving plants are chiefly to be found in rich, black, swampy mould, beneath the shade of trees and rank herbage, near creeks and damp places, in or about the forest.

The sheath that envelops and protects the spadix, or central portion of the plant, is an incurved membraneous hood of a pale green colour, beautifully striped with dark purple or brownish-purple.

The flowers are inconspicuous, hidden by the sheath; they are of two kinds, the sterile and fertile, the former placed above, the latter consisting of four or more stamens and 2 4-celled anthers, the fertile or fruit-bearing flowers of a 1-celled OVARY. The fruit, when ripe, is bright scarlet, clustered round the lower part of the round fleshy scape. As the berries ripen, the hood or sheath withers and shrivels away to admit the ripening rays of heat and light to the fruit.

The root of the Indian Turnip consists of a round, wrinkled, fleshy corm, somewhat larger than that of the garden crocus; from this rises the simple scape or stem of the plant, which is sheathed with the base of the leaves. These are on long naked stalks, divided into three ovate pointed leaflets, waved at the edges.

The juices of the Indian Turnip are hot, acrid, and of a poisonous quality, but can be rendered useful and harmless by the action of heat; the roots roasted in the fire are no longer poisonous. The Indian herbalists use the Indian Turnip in medicine as a remedy in violent colic, long experience having taught them in what manner to employ this dangerous root.

The Arum belongs to a natural order, most plants of which contain an acrid poison, yet under proper care can be made valuable articles of food. Among these we may mention the roots of *Colocosia mucronatum, Violaceum,* and others, which, under the more familiar names of EDDOES and YAMS, are in common use in tropical countries.

The juice of *Arum triphyllum,* our Indian Turnip, has been used, boiled in milk, as a remedy for consumption.

Portland sago is prepared from the larger species, *Arum maculatum,* Spotted Arum. The corm, or root, yields a fine, white, starchy powder, similar to Arrow-root, and is prepared much in the same way as potato starch. The pulp, after being ground or pounded, is thrown into clean water and stirred; the water, after settling, is poured off, and the white sediment is again submitted to the same process until it becomes quite pure, and is then dried. A pound of this starch may be made from a peck of the roots. The roots should be dried in sand before using. Thus purified and divested of its poisonous qualities, the powder so procured becomes a pleasant and valuable article of food, and is sold under the name of Portland Sago, or Portland Arrow-root.

When deprived of the poisonous acrid juices that pervade them, all our known species may be rendered valuable both as food and medicine; but they should not be employed without care and experience. The writer remembers, not many years ago, several children being poisoned by the leaves of Arum triphyllum being gathered and eaten as greens in one of the early-settled back townships of Western Canada. The same deplorable accident happened by ignorant persons gathering the leaves of the Mandrake or May Apple (*Podophyllin pedatum*).

There seems in the vegetable world, as well as in the moral, two opposite principles, the good and the evil. The gracious God has given to man the power, by the cultivation of his intellect, to elicit the good and useful, separating it from the vile and injurious, thus turning that into a blessing which would otherwise be a curse.

" The Arum family possess many valuable medicinal qualities," says Dr. Charles Lee, in his valuable work on the medicinal plants of North America, "but would nevertheless become dangerous poisons in the hands of ignorant persons."

The useful Cassava, (*Zanipha Manipor*), of the West Indies and tropical America, is another remarkable instance of art overcoming nature, and obtaining a positive good from that which in its natural state is evil. The cassava, from the flour of which the bread made by the natives is manufactured, being the starchy parts of a poisonous plant of the Euphorbia family, the milky juice of which is highly acrid and poisonous. The pleasant and useful article sold in the shops under the name of tapioca is also made from the Cassava root.

NAT. ORD. ORCHIDACEÆ.

Showy Orchis.

Orchis Spectabilis.

"Full many a gem of purest ray serene,
  The dark unfathomed caves of ocean bear;
Full many a flower is born to blush unseen,
  And waste its sweetness on the desert air."

GRAY.

DEEP hidden in the damp recesses of the leafy woods, many a rare and precious flower of the Orchis family blooms, flourishes, and decays, unseen by human eye, unsought by human hand, until some curious, flower-loving botanist plunges amid the rank, tangled vegetation, and brings beauties to the light.

One of these beautiful Orchids, the *Orchis spectabile* or SHOWY ORCHIS, is here presented in our group.

This pretty plant is not, indeed, of very rare occurrence; its locality is rich maple and beechen woods all through Canada. The colour of the flower is white, shaded, and spotted with pink or purplish lilac; the corolla is what is termed ringent or throated, the upper petals and sepals arching over the hollow lower-lipped petal. The scape is smooth and fleshy, terminating in a loosely-flowered and many-bracted spike; the bracts are dark-green, sharp-pointed, and leafy; the root a bundle of round white fibres; the leaves, two in number, are large, blunt, oblong, shining, smooth, and oily, from three to five inches long, one larger than the other. The flowering time of the species is May and June.

Our forest glades and boggy swamps hide many a rare and precious flower known but to few; among some of the most beautiful of this interesting group of plants, we might direct attention to the elegant and rare Calypso borealis, Pogonia triphoria, and Pogonia pendula. The beautiful Grass Pink, *Calopogon pulchellus*, with many others of the Orchidaceæ tribe, may be regarded as flower gems to be prized alike for their exquisite forms and colouring as for their scarcity.

These lovely Orchids, transplanted to the greenhouse or conservatory, would be regarded as objects of great interest, but are rarely seen and little valued by the careless passer-by, if he chances upon them in their forest haunts.

Painted Cup, Scarlet Cup.

Castillèia Coccinea.

> Scarlet tufts
> Are glowing in the green like flakes of fire;
> The wanderers of the prairie know them well,
> And call that brilliant flower the Painted Cup.
>
> BRYANT.

THIS splendidly-coloured plant is the glory and ornament of the plain-lands of Canada. The whole plant is a glow of scarlet, varying from pale flame-colour to the most vivid vermillion, rivalling in brilliancy of hues the scarlet geranium of the greenhouse.

The Painted Cup owes its gay appearance not to its flowers, which are not very conspicuous at a distance, but to the deeply-cut leafy tracts that enclose them and clothe the stalks, forming at the ends of the flower branches clustered rosettes. (See our artist's plate.)

The flower is a flattened tube, bordered with bright red, and edged with golden yellow. Stamens, four; pistil, one, projecting beyond the tube of the calix; the capsule is many seeded. The radical or root leaves are of a dull, hoary green, tinged with reddish purple, as also is the stem, which is rough, hairy, and angled. The bracts, or leafy appendages, which appear on the *lower* part of the stalk, are but slightly tinged with scarlet, but the colour deepens and brightens towards the middle and summit of the branched stem.

The Scarlet Cup appears in May, along with the smaller white and red trilliums; but these early plants are small; the stem simple, rarely branched, and the colour of a deeper red. As the summer advances, our gallant soldier-like plant puts on all its bravery of attire. All through the glowing harvest months, the open grassy plains and the borders of the cultivated fields are enriched by its glorious colours. In favourable soils the plant rises, enclosed in a tubular *slightly* twice-cleft calyx, of a pale green colour, attains a height of from 2ft. 4in., throwing out many side branches, terminated by the clustered, brilliantly-tinted bracts; some heads being as large as a medium-sized rose. They have been gathered in the corners of the stubble fields on the cultivated plains, as late as October. A not uncommon slender variety occurs of a pale buff, and also of a bright lemon colour. The American botanists speak of *Castillèia coccinea*, as being addicted to a low, wettish soil, but it is not so with our Canadian plant; if you would find it in its greatest perfection, you must seek it on the high, dry, rolling plains of Rice-lake, Brantford, to the north of Toronto, Stoney lake, the neighbourhood of Peterboro, and similar localities; it is neither to be found in swamps nor in the shade of the uncleared forest.

For soil, the Scarlet Cup seems to prefer light loam, and evidently courts the sunshine rather than the shade. If it could be prevailed upon to flourish in our garden borders, it would be a great acquisition, from its long flowering time and its brilliant colouring.

1. PYROLA ELLIPTICA. 2. MONESES UNIFLOEA. 3. RUBUS ODORATUS. 4. VERONICA AMERICANA.
(Shin Leaf.) (One-flowered Pyrola.) (Purple flowering Raspberry.) (American Brooklime.)

PAINTED CUP, SCARLET CUP.

These lovely plants, like many others that adorn our Canadian woods and wilds, yearly disappear from our midst, and soon we shall seek them, but not find them.

We might say with the poet:

> " 'Twas pity nature brought ye forth,
> Merely to show your worth,
> And lose ye quite!
> But ye have lovely leaves, where we
> May read how soon things have
> Their end, though ne'er so brave;
> And after they have shewn their pride,
> Like you awhile they glide
> Into the grave.
>
> HERRICK.

NAT. ORD. COMPOSITÆ.

Cone Flower.

Rudbéckia fulgida.

THE Cone Flower is one of the handsomest of our rayed flowers. The gorgeous flaming orange dress, with the deep purple disk of almost metallic lustre, is one of the ornaments of all our wild open prairies-like plains during the hot months of July, August and September. We find the Cone-Flower on the sunny spots among the wild herbage of grassy thickets, associated with the wild Sunflowers, Asters and other plants of the widely diffused Composite Order.

During the harvest months, when the more delicate spring flowers are ripening their seed, our heat-loving Rudbeckias, Chrysanthemums, Sun-flowers, Coreopsises, Ox-eyes, and Asters, are lifting their starry heads to greet the light and heat of the sun's ardent rays, adorning the dry wastes, gravelly and sandy hills, and wide grassy plains, with their gay blossoms;

> "Bright flowers that linger as they fall,
> Whose last are dearest."

Many of these compound flowers possess medicinal qualities. Some, as the thistle, dandelion, wild lettuce, and others, are narcotic, being supplied with an abundance of bitter milky juice. The

Sun-flower, Coreopsis, Cone-flower, Tagweed, and Tansy, contain resinous properties.

The beautiful Aster family, if not remarkable for any peculiarly useful qualities, contains many highly ornamental plants. Numerous species of these charming flowers belong to our Canadian flora; lingering with us

"When fairer flowers are all decayed,"

brightening the waste places and banks of lakes and lonely streams with starry flowers of every hue and shade—white, pearly blue, and deep purple; while the Solidagoes (Aaron's rod), are celebrated for the valuable dyes that are yielded by their deep golden blossoms. But to return to the subject of our artist's plate, the Cone Flower.

The plant is from one to three feet in height, the stem simple, or branching, each branchlet terminating in a single head. The rays are of a deep orange colour, varying to yellow; the leaves broadly lanceolate, sometimes once or twice lobed, partly clasping the rough, hairy stem, hoary and of a dull green, few and scattered. The scales of the chaffy disk are of a dark, shining purple, forming a somewhat depressed cone. This species, with a slenderer-stemmed variety, with rays of a golden yellow, are to be met with largely diffused over the Province.

Many splendid species of the Cone Flower are to be found in the wide-spread prairies of the Western States, where their brilliant starry flowers are mingled with many a gay blossom known only to the wild Indian hunter, and the herb-seeking medicine men of the native tribes, who know their medicinal and healing qualities, if they are insensible to their outward beauties.

Nat. Ord. Ericaceæ.—Sub. Ord. Pyroleæ.

Sweet Wintergreen.

Pýrola ellíptica.

THE familiar name "Wintergreen" is applied by the Canadians to many species of dwarf evergreen plants without any reference to their natural affinities. The beautiful family of Pyrolas share this name in common with many other charming forest flowers in reference to their evergreen habit.

Every member of this interesting family is worthy of special notice. Elegant in form and colouring, of a delicate fragrance and enduring verdure, they add to their many attractions the merit of being almost the first green thing to refresh the eye long wearied by gazing on the dazzling snow for many consecutive months of winter.

As the dissolving crust disappears from the forest beneath the kindly influence of the transient sunbeams of early spring, the deep glossy-green shoots of the hardy Pyrolas peep forth, not timidly, as if afraid to meet

"The snow and blinding sleet;"

not shrinking from the chilling blast that too often nips the fair promise of April and May, but boldly and cheerfully braving the worst that the capricious season has in store for such early risers.

All bright, and fresh, and glossy, our Wintergreens come forth as though they had been perfecting their toilet within the sheltering canopy of their snowy chambers, to do honour to the new-born year just awakening from her icy sleep.

P. ELLÍPTICA forms extensive beds in the forest, the roots creeping with running subterranean shoots which send up clusters of evergreen leaves, slightly waved and scalloped at the edges, of a deep glossy green and thin in texture.

The name Pyrola is derived from a fancied likeness in the foliage to that of the Pear, but this is not very obvious, nevertheless we will not cavil at it, for it is a pretty sounding word, far better than many one that has been bestowed upon our showy wild flowers, in compliment to the person that first brought them into notice.

The pale-greenish white flower of our Pyrola forms a tall terminal raceme, the five round petals are hollow; each blossom set on a slender pedicle, at the base of which is a small pointed bract; the anthers are of a reddish orange colour, the stamens ascending in a cluster, while the long style is declined, forming a figure somewhat like the letter J. The seed vessel is ribbed berry-shaped, slightly flattened and turbinate; when dry, the light chaffy seeds escape through valves at the sides. The dry style in this and most of the genus remain persistent on the capsule.

The number 5 prevails in this plant; the calyx is 5 parted; petals 5; stamens 10, or twice five; stigma one, but 5 rayed; 5 knobs or tubercles at the apex; seed-vessel 5 celled and 5 valved. The flowers are generally from 5 to 10 on the scape. Most of our Pyrolas are remarkable for the rich fragrance of their flowers, especially *P. rotundifòlia*, *P. ellíptica*, *P. incarnàta*, and *P. minor*.

SWEET WINTERGREEN.

These flowers are, for the most part, found in rich woods, some in low wet ground, but a few prefer the drier soil of piny forests, and one of the finest and most fragrant of the species grows freely on grassy uplands. The larger flowered P. rotundifòlia (round-leaved Pyrola). The exquisitely beautiful evergreen plant known by Canadian settlers as *Prince's Pine* is a member of the family of Pyrola.

From root to summit this plant is altogether lovely. The leaves are dark, shining and smooth, evergreen and finely serrated; the stem of a bright rosy-red; the delicately pink-tinted flowers look as if moulded from wax; the anthers are of a bright amethyst-purple, set round the emerald-green turbinated stigma. The flowers are not many, but form a loose corymb springing from the centre of the shining green leaves. There is scarcely a more attractive native plant than the *Chimáphila umbellàta* in our Canadian flora.

The leaves of this beautiful Wintergreen are held in high estimation by the Indian herbalists who call it RHEUMATISM WEED, (*Pipissewa*.) It is bitter and aromatic in quality.

NAT. ORD. ERICACEÆ.—SUB. ORD. PYROLEÆ.

One Flowered Pyrola.

Monèses uniflorà.

THIS exquisitely scented flower is only found in the shade of the forest, in rich black leaf mould, where, like P. elliptica, it forms considerable beds; it is of evergreen habit. The leaves are of a dark green and smooth surface, clustered at the base of the running root-stork and sending up from the centre one simple scape, bearing a gracefully nodding flower; each milk-white petal is elegantly scalloped; the stamens, 8 to 10, are set close to the base of the petal; the anthers are of a bright purple amethyst colour; the style straight, with five radiating points at the extremity forming a perfect mural crown in shape; it is of a bright green and much exceeds in length the stamen.

The scent of the flower is very fine, resembling in richness that of the hyacinthe. This species is not common. There is another variety of the single-flowered Pyrola that is of more frequent occurrence in our woods. The flower is of a greenish white, the anthers of a brownish fawn colour, the whole height of the plant scarcely exceeding four or five inches, and the scent is less fragrant than that of the pure white single Pyrola (*Monèses uniflorà.*)

1. ERYTHRONIUM AMERICANUM.   2. TRILLIUM GRANDIFLORUM.   3. AQUILEGIA CANADENSIS.
(Yellow adder's tongue.)   (Large white Trillium.)   (Wild Columbine.)

NAT. ORD. ROSACEÆ.

Flowering Raspberry.

Rùbus Odoràtus.

IN English gardens our beautiful Red-Flowered, Sweet-Scented Raspberry is deemed worthy of a place in the shrubberies, but in its native country it is passed by because it is not an exotic, and therefore regarded as of little worth.—Like a prophet it has no honour in its own country.—Yet what can be more lovely than its rose-shaped blossoms, from the deep purplish-crimson bud wrapped in its odorous mossy calyx, to the unfolded flower of various shades of deep rose and paler reddish lilac. The flowers of the Red Raspberry derive their pleasant aromatic odour from the closely-set coating of short bristly glandular hairs, each one of which is tipped with a gland of reddish hue, containing a sweet-scented gum, as in the mossy envelope of the moss-rose of the garden. These appendages, seen by the aid of a powerful microscope, are objects of exquisite beauty, more admirable than rubies and diamonds, living gems that fill us with wonder while we gaze into their marvellous parts and glorious colours.

All through the hot months of June, July and August, a succession of flowers are put forth at the ends of the branches and branchlets of our Sweet Raspberry—

"An odorous chaplet of sweet summer buds."

The shrub is from two to five feet in height, branching from the woody perennial root-stock; the leaves are from three to five lobed, the lobes pointed and roughly toothed. The leaves are of a dullish green, varying in size from several inches to mere bracts. The blossoms are often as large as those of the sweet-briar and dog-rose, but when first unfolded more compact and cup like. The fruit consists of many small red grains, somewhat dry and acid, scarcely tempting to the palate, but not injurious in any degree. The shrub is more attractive for its flowers than its insipid fruit. We have indeed few that are more ornamental among our native plants than the RUBUS ODORATUS. Canada cannot boast of the Rhododendrons and Azaleas that adorn the Western and Northern States, but she possesses many attractive shrubs that are but little known, which flourish year after year on the lonely shores of our inland lakes and marshy beaver-meadows, Ledums and Kalmias, with many a fair flower that withers unnoticed and uncared for in its solitary native haunts.

Speedwell.

AMERICAN BROOKLIME.

Veronica Americàna.

"Flowers spring up and die ungathered."

IN the language of flowers the blossoms of the Veronica or Speedwell are said to mean undying love, or constancy, but the blossoms of the Speedwell are fugacious, falling quickly, and therefore, one would say, not a good emblem of endurance.

Sweet simple flowers are the wild Veronicas, chiefly inhabiting damp overflowed ground, the borders of weedy ponds and brooks, from whence the names of "Brooklime" and "Marsh Speedwell," "Water Speedwell," and the like. Some of the species are indeed found mostly growing on dry hills and grassy banks, cheering the eye of the passing traveller by its slender spikes of azure flowers, and this is often known by the pretty name of Forget-me-not, though it is not the true "Forget-me-not," which is *Myosotis palustris*, also called "SCORPION-GRASS;" the derivation of which last name we should find it difficult to trace.

The subject of the elegant little flower on the right hand side of the plate is *Veronica Americàna*—"AMERICAN BROOKLIME"—one of the prettiest of the native Veronicas, and may easily be recognized by its branching spikes of blue flowers, and veiny, partially heart-shaped leaves.

NAT. ORD. LILIACEÆ.

Adders-Tongue.

DOG-TOOTHED VIOLET.

Erythrònium Americánum.

"And spotted Adders-tongue with drooping bell,
Greeting the new-born spring."

IN rich black mould, on the low banks of creeks and open woodlands, large beds of these elegant lilies may be seen piercing the softened ground in the month of April; the broad lanceolate leaves are beautifully clouded with purple or reddish brown, or sometimes with milky white. Each bulb of the *second* year's growth produces two leaves, and between these rises a round naked scape, (or flower-stem), terminated by a drooping yellow bell. The unfolded bud is striped with lines of dark purple. A few hours of sunshine and warm wind soon expands the flower, which is composed of six coloured sepals,* recurved which form a lily-like turbaned flower; each segment grooved, and spotted at the base, with oblong purplish brown dots. The outer surface of the sepals are marked with dark lines. The stamens are

---

* *Sepals* are the leaves of the *calyx*; in liliaceous flowers the calyx and corolla being not obviously distinguishable, the name *perianth* is often applied to the whole; but really there are three sepals—the outer circle, and three petals—the inner circle—to call them all sepals is incorrect.—PROF. HINCKS.

six; anthers, oblong; pollen of a brick-red, or dull orange colour, varying to yellow. The style is club-shaped; stigmas three, united.

This elegant yellow lily bends downward when expanded, as if to hide its glories from the full glare of the sun-light. The clouded leaves are of an oily smoothness, resisting the moisture of rain and dew.

The name Dogs-tooth Violet seems very inappropriate. The pointed segments of the bell may have suggested the resemblance to the tooth of a dog, but it is difficult to trace any analogy between this flower and the violet, no two plants presenting greater dissimilarity of form or habit than the lily and the violet, though often blended in the verse of the poet. The American name of the Adders-tongue is more significant.*

The White Flowered Adders-tongue grows it has been said in the more western portion of Canada, on the shores of Lake Huron, probably the *Erythrònium álbidum* of Gray.

---

* The name Dogs-tooth refers to the shape of the small pointed white bulbs of the common European species, so well known in English gardens.—PROF. LAWSON.

Sub Ord. Trilliàceæ.—(Trillium Family.)

White Trillium.

DEATH FLOWER.

Tríllium Grandiflòrum.

"And spotless lilies bend the head
 Low to the passing gale."

NATURE has scattered with no niggardly hand these remarkable flowers over hill and dale, wide shrubby plain and shady forest glen. In deep ravines, on rocky islets, the bright snow white blossoms of the Trilliums greet the eye and court the hand to pluck them. The old people in this part of the Province call them by the familiar name of Lily. Thus we have *Asphodel Lilies, Douro Lilies, &c.* In Nova Scotia they are called Moose-flowers, probably from being abundant in the haunts of Moose-deer. In some of the New England States the Trilliums, white and red, are known as the *Death-flower*, but of the origin of so ominous a name we have no record. We might imagine it to have originated in the use of the flower to deck the coffin or graves of the dead in the olden times. The pure white blossoms of T. nivàle, T. cérnuum (nodding Trillium) and T. grandiflòrum, might serve not inappropriately for emblems of innocence and purity, when laid upon the breast of the early dead. The darker and more sanguine hue of the red species, T. *sessile*, and T. *recurvàtum*, might have been selected for such as fell by violence, but these are but conjecture. A prettier name has been given to the Nodding Trillium: that of "Smiling Wake-robin," which seems to be associated with the coming of the cheerful chorister of early spring, "The household bird with the red stomacher," as Bishop Carey calls the robin red-breast. The botanical name of the Trillium is derived from trilex, triple, all the parts of the plant being in threes. Thus we see the round fleshy scape furnished with three large sad green leaves, closely set round the stem; two or three inches below the flower; which is composed of a calyx of *three* sepals, a corolla of *three* large snow white, or, else, chocolate red petals: the styles or stigmas *three;* ovary *three* celled; stamens *six*, which is a reproduction of three. The white fleshy tuberous root is much used by the American School of Medicine in various diseases, also by the Indian herb doctors.

Trillium grandiflòrum is the largest and most showy of the white species. *Trillium nivàle* or "lesser snowy Trillium," is the smallest; this last blooms *early* in May. May and June are the months in which these flowers appear. The white flowered trilliums are subject to many varieties, and accidental alterations. The green of the sepals is often transferred to the white petals in T. nivàle; some are found handsomely striped with red and green, and in others the very short foot-stalk of the almost sessile leaves are lengthened into long petioles. The large White Trillium is changed previous to its fading to a dull reddish lilac.

The Red Trilliums are rich but sombre in colour, the petals are longish-ovate, regular, not waved, and the pollen is of a greyish dusty

1. DICENTRA CANADENSIS.   2. TRILLIUM ERECTUM.   4. TRIENTALIS AMERICANA.
(Squirrel Corn.)   (Purple trillium.)   (Star flower Chickweed.)

3. GERANIUM MACULATUM.
(Wild Crane's bill.)

hue, while that of the White species is bright orange-yellow. The leaves are of a dark lurid green, the colouring matter of the petals seems to pervade the leaves; and here, let me observe, that the same remark may be made of many other plants. In purple flowers we often perceive the violet hue to be perceptible in the stalk and under part of the leaves, and sometimes in the veins and roots. Red flowers again show the same tendency in stalk and veins.

The Blood-root in its early stage of growth shews the Orange juice in the stem and leaves, so does the Canadian Balsam, and many others; that, a little observation will point out. The colouring matter of flowers has always been, more or less, a mystery to us: that light is one of the great agents can hardly for a moment be doubted, but something also may depend upon the peculiar quality of the juices that fill the tissues of the flower, and on the cellular tissue itself. Flowers deprived of light we know are pallid and often colourless, but how do we account for the deep crimson of the beet-root, the rose-red of the radish, the orange of the rhubarb, carrot, and turnip, which roots, being buried in the earth, are not subject to the solar rays? The natural supposition would be that all roots hidden from the light would be white, but this is by no means the case. The question is one of much interest and deserves the attention of all naturalists, and especially of the botanical student.

Nat. Ord. Ranunculaceæ.

Rock Columbine.

Aquilègia Canadénsis.

"The graceful columbine all blushing red,
  Bends to the earth her crown
  Of honey-laden bells."

THIS graceful flower enlivens us all through the months of May and June by its brilliant blossoms of deep red and golden yellow.

In general outline the Wild Columbine resembles its cultivated sisters of the garden, but is more light and airy from its nodding habit. The plant throws up many tall slender stalks from its centre, furnished with leafy bracts, from which spring other light stems terminated by little pedicels, each bearing a large drooping flower and bud which open in succession.

The flower consists of five red sepals and five red petals; the latter are hollowed trumpet-like at the mouth, ascending; they form narrow tubes, which are terminated by little round knobs filled with honey. The delicate thready pedicels on which the blossom hangs cause it to droop down and thus throw up the honey bearing tubes of the petals; the little balls forming a pretty sort of floral coronet at the junction with the stalk.

The unequal and clustered stamens, and five thready styles of the pistil project beyond the hollow mouths of the petals, like an elegant golden fringed tassel; the edges and interior of the petals are also of a bright golden yellow. These gay colours are well contrasted with the deep green of the root leaves and bracts of the flower stalks. The bracts are lobed in two or three divisions. The larger leaves are placed on long foot stalks, each leaf is divided into three, which are again twice or thrice lobed, and unequally notched; the upper surface is smooth and of a dark rich green, the under pale and whitish.

As the flowers fade the husky hollow seed pods become erect— a wise provision in this and many other plants of drooping habits, giving the ripening seed better access to the sun and wind and preventing them from being prematurely scattered abroad upon the earth.

The wild Columbine is perennial and very easily cultivated Its blossoms are eagerly sought out by the bees and humming birds. On sunny days you may be sure to see the latter hovering over the bright drooping bells, extracting the rich nectar with which they are so bountifully supplied. Those who care for bees, and love humming birds, should plant the graceful red-flowered Columbine in their garden borders.

In its wild state it is often found growing among rocks and surface stones, where it insinuates its roots into the clefts and hollows that are filled with rich vegetable mould; and thus, being often seen adorning the sterile rocks with its bright crown of waving blossoms, it has obtained the name in some places of ROCK COLUMBINE.

NAT. ORD. FUMARIACEÆ.—(FUMITORY FAMILY.)

Squirrel Corn.

Dicéntra Canadénsis.

THIS graceful plant belongs to the fumitory family, of which we have many cultivated varieties in Britain and elsewhere. Here our lovely flower grows wild in rich black mould in the forest, and in recently cleared spots within its protecting shadow, where its drooping bells and rich scent have gained for it the not very inappropriate name of "WILD HYACINTH." The common name of "Squirrel-Corn" is derived from the round orange tubers at the roots, resembling in size and colour grains of Indian-Corn, and from their being a favourite food with the ground squirrel.

The blossoms are of a pellucid whiteness, sometimes tinged with reddish lilac; they form a drooping raceme on a round smooth scape, springing from a scaly bud; the corolla is heart shaped, composed of four petals, in two pairs, flattened and sac-like, the tips united over the stigma, and slightly projecting; in *D. cucullària* assuming the likeness of the head of a fly, the cream coloured diverging petals presenting a strong resemblance to the deer-fly of our lakes. This very charming species is known by the somewhat vulgar name of "BREECHES FLOWER" and "DUTCHMAN'S BREECHES." A more descriptive name would be "FLY-FLOWER."

All the species flourish under cultivation, and become very ornamental early border flowers; but care should be taken to plant them in rich black vegetable mould, the native soil of their forest haunts.

Our artist has chosen the delicate rosy-tinted variety as the subject of the left-hand flower of the plate.

Purple Trillium.

DEATH-FLOWER.—BIRTH-ROOT.

Tríllium eréctum.

"Bring flowers, bring flowers o'er the bier to shed
A crown for the brow of the early dead.
Though they smile in vain for what once was ours,
They are love's last gift, bring flowers, bring flowers."

HEMANS.

GRAY and other botanical writers call this striking flower (T. eréctum) the "*Purple Tríllium;*" it should rather be called RED, its hue being decidedly more *red* than purple, and in the New England States it is called by the country folks, "The Red Death-Flower," in contrast to the larger White Tríllium, or "WHITE DEATH-FLOWER." For further remarks on this singular name we refer the reader to the description of that flower where all the native varieties of the genus are dwelt upon, including the one now before us, which forms the central flower in the present group, and shall merely add that like the rest of this remarkable family, *T. eréctum* is widely spread over the whole of Canada. It appears in the middle of May and continues blooming till June, preferring the soil of rich shady woods.

"Few of our indigenous plants surpass the Trillium in elegance and beauty, and they are all endowed with valuable medicinal properties. The root of the Purple Trillium is generally believed to be the most active. Tannin and Bitter Extract form two of its most remarkable ingredients." So says that intelligent writer on the medicinal plants of North America, Dr. Charles Lee. There are three of the dark flowered Trillium enumerated by Gray, two of which appear to be common to our Canadian soil, T. eréctum and T. sessile. The latter is smaller, and often the dull chocolate colour of the pointed petals assumes a livid greenish hue. It is earlier in flowering, appearing at the beginning of May, at the same time with T. niv àle, the "Dwarf White" or "SNOWY TRÍLLIUM."

Under cultivation the flowers of all the species become very ornamental; they require black leaf mould and moderate shade, and, if left to grow undisturbed, increase and continue to flower, year after year, in the borders or shrubbery.

The seeds when ripe are easily obtained; they are hard and bony, several in each division of the three celled capsule. The roots of these plants are thick, wrinkled, fleshy, and contain the medicinal principle described by Dr. Lee.

4. VACCINIUM OXYCOCCUS. 3. IRIS VERSICOLOR. 2. CYPRIPEDIUM PUBESCENS. 1. CYPRIPEDIUM PARVIFLORUM.
(Small Cranberry.) (Larger blue Flag.) (Larger yellow Lady's Slipper.) (Smaller Lady's Slipper.)

NAT. ORD.—GERANIACEÆ.

Wood Gerànium.

CRANES-BILL.

(Gerànium maculàtum.)

THERE are but few flowers of the Cranes-bill family in Canada. The one most worthy of notice is the Wood Gerànium (*Gerànium maculàtum*). This is a very ornamental plant; its favourite locality is open grassy thickets among low bushes, especially those tracts of country known as Oak-openings, where it often reaches to the height of from 2° to 3°, throwing out many branches adorned with deep lilac flowers; the half-opened buds are very lovely. The blossom consists of five petals, obtuse and slightly indented on their upper margins, and are lined and delicately veined with purple. The calyx consists of five pointed sepals; stamens ten; the anthers are of a reddish brown; styles five, cohering at the top. When the seed is mature these curl up bearing the ripe brown seed adhering to the base of each one. The common name Cranes-bill has been derived from the long grooved and stork-like beak which supports the styles. The Greek name of the plant means a Crane. The whole plant is more or less beset with silvery hairs. The leaves are divided into about five principal segments; these again are lobed and cut into sharply pointed irregularly sized teeth.

The larger hairy root leaves are often discoloured with red and purplish blotches from whence the specific name (*maculàtum*), spotted, has been given by botanists to this species.

The flower stem is much branched and furnished with leafy bracts; the principal flowers are on long stalks, usually three springing from a central branch and again subdividing into smaller branchlets terminating in buds mostly in threes, on drooping slender pedicels; as the older and larger blossoms fall off a fresh succession appears on the side branches, furnishing rather smaller but equally beautiful flowers during many weeks. Gray gives the blooming season of the Cranes-bill from April to July, but with us it rarely appears before June, and may be seen all through July and August.

This Wood Geranium is a beautiful species, and would no doubt repay the trouble of cultivation. Besides being very ornamental our plant possesses virtues which are well known to the herbalist as powerful astringents, which quality has obtained for it the name of '*Alum root*,' among the country people, who apply a decoction of the root as a styptic for wounds; and sweetened, as a gargle for sore throats and ulcerated mouth: it is also given to young children to correct a lax state of the system.

Thus our plant is remarkable for its usefulness as well as for its beauty.

A showy species, with large rose-coloured flowers and much dissected leaves, may be found on some of the rocky islets in Stoney Lake, Ont. The slender flower stem is about six inches in height, springing from a leafy involucre which is cut and divided into many long and narrow segments; flowers generally from one to three, terminal on the little bracted-foot-stalks. The seed vessels not so long as in the Wood Geranium.

Besides the above named we have two smaller species. The well known HERB ROBERT—*G. robertiànum* or feotid geranium—which is said to have been introduced from Britain, but is by no means uncommon in Canada, in half cleared woodlands and by waysides attracting the eye by its bright pink flowers, and elegantly cut leaves, which becomes bright red in the fall of the year. This pretty species is renowned for its rank and disagreeable odour when handled.

Another small flowered specie, with pale insignificant blossoms is also common as a weed by road sides and in open woods, probably this is *G. pusíllum*, smaller Cranes-bill; it also resembles the British plant, but is of too frequent occurrence in remote localities to lead us to suppose it to be otherwise than a native production of the soil.

NAT. ORD. PRIMULACEÆ.

Chickweed Wintergreen.

Trientàlis.

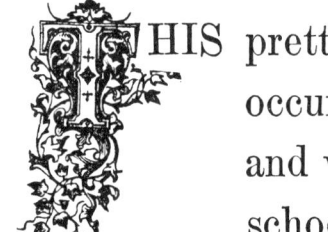HIS pretty starry-flowered little plant is remarkable for the occurrence of the number seven in its several parts, and was for some time regarded by botanists of the old school as the representative of the Class Heptandria.

The calyx is seven parted; the divisions of the delicate white corolla also seven; and the stamens seven. The leaves form a whorl at the upper part of the stem, mostly from five to seven, or eight; the leaves are narrow, tapering at both ends, of a delicate light-green, thin in texture, and of a pleasant sub-acid flavour. The star-shaped flowers, few in number, on thread-like stalks, rise from the centre of the whorl of leaves, which thus form an involucre to the pretty delicate starry flowers. This little plant is frequently found at the roots of beech-trees; it is fond of shade, and in light vegetable mould forms considerable beds; the roots are white, slender, and fibrous; it is one of our early May flowers, though, unless the month be warm and genial, will delay its opening somewhat later. In old times, when the herbalists gave all kinds of fanciful names to the wild plants, they would have bestowed such a name as "Herbe Innocence" upon our modest little forest flower.

NAT. ORD. ORCHIDACEÆ.

Yellow Lady's Slippers.

Cypripèdium parviflòrum and Cypripèdium pubéscens.

"And golden slippers meet for Faries' feet."

THIS ornamental family are remarkable alike for the singular beauty of their flowers, and the peculiar arrangement of the internal organs. In the Linnæan classification they were included in common, with all the Orchis tribe, in the class Gynandria, but in the Natural Order of Jussieu, which we have followed, the "Lady's Slipper" (*Cypripèdium*), forms one of the sub-orders in the general Order ORCHIDACEÆ.

Of the two species represented in our Artist's group, the larger and central flower is *Cypripèdium pubéscens*, the smaller, *C. parviflòrum*, or LESSER LADY'S SLIPPER. The latter is, perhaps, the more elegant and graceful plant, and is also somewhat fragrant. The sepals and petals are longer and more spiral, but the colouring of the lip is not so rich and vivid as in the larger flower, *C. Pubéscens.*

The small flowered plant affects a moist soil, such as low wet meadows and open swampy woods; while the larger species, better known by its more familiar name Moccasin flower, loves the open woodlands and drier plains; where, in the month of June, it may be seen beside the gay Painted Cup (*Castillèia coccínea*), the Blue Lupine (*L. perénnis*), the larger White Trillium, and other lovely wild flowers, forming a charming contrast to their various colours and no less varied forms.

The stem of the larger Moccasin flower is thick and leafy, each bright green, many-nerved leaf sheathing the flowers before they open. The flowers are from one to three in number; bent forward; drooping gracefully downwards. The golden sac-like lip is elegantly striped and spotted with ruby red; the twisted narrow petals, and sepals, two in number of each kind, are of a pale fawn colour, sometimes veined and lined with a deeper shade. Like many others of the genus, the organs of the flower assume a singular and grotesque resemblance to the face of some animal. On lifting up the fleshy petal-like middle lobe which protects the stamens and pistil, the face of an Indian hound may be imagined; the stamens, which are two in number, situated one on either side of the sterile depressed central lobe, when the flower is mature, turn of a deep brown, and resemble two round eyes; the blunt stigma takes the form of the nose, while the sepals look like ears. There is something positively comical in the appearance of the ape-like face of *C. spectábile*, the beautiful showy Lady's Slipper, the description of which will be found to face the plate in which it forms a prominent feature.

The most beautiful of all the species is the "STEMLESS LADY'S SLIPPER," *Cypripèdium Acaùle*, of which we will treat at some future time. It bears removal to the garden if planted in a suitable situation; but all these native flowers require attention to their peculiar habits and soil, or they will disappoint the expectation of the cultivator and end in failure. All wild flowers transplanted from the woods require shade, and bog plants both moisture and shade.

NAT. ORD. IRIDACEÆ.

Large Blue Flag.

Iris Versicolor. Fleur-de-luce.

Lilies of all kinds,
The fleur-de-luce being one.

WINTER'S TALE.

THIS beautiful flower, the blue Iris, which forms the left hand figure in the group of Moccasin flowers, abounds all through Canada, and forms one of the ornaments of our low sandy flats, marshy meadows and over-flowed lake shores; it delights in wet muddy soil, and often forms large clumps of verdure in half-dried up ponds and similar localities. Early in spring, as soon as the sun has warmed the waters after the melting of the ice, the sharp sword-shaped leaves escaping from the sheltering sheath that enfolded them, pierce the moist ground, and appear, forming beds of brilliant verdure, concealing the swampy soil and pools of stagnant water below. Late in the month of June the bursting buds of rich purple begin to unfold, peeping through the spathe that envelopes them. A few days of sunshine, and the graceful petals, so soft and silken in texture, so variable in shades of colour, unfold: the three outer ones reflexed, droop gracefully downwards, while the three innermost, which are of paler tint, sharper and stiffer, stand erect and conceal the stamens and petal-like stigmas, which lie behind them: an arrangement so suitable for the preservation of the fructifying organs of the flower, that we cannot fail to behold in it the wisdom of the great Creator. The structure of the cellular tissue in most water plants, and the smooth oily surface of their leaves, has also been provided as a means of throwing off the moisture to which their place of growth must necessarily expose them; but for this wise provision, which keeps the surface dry though surrounded with water, the plants would become overcharged with moisture and rot and decay too rapidly to perfect the ripening of their seeds—a process often carried on at the bottom of streams and lakes, as in the case of the Pond-lily and other aquatics. Our blue Iris, however, does not follow this rule, being only partly an aquatic, but stands erect and ripens the large bony, three-sided seeds in a three-sided membraneous pod. The hard seeds of the *Iris versicolor* have been roasted and used as a substitute for coffee. The root, which is creeping, fleshy and tuberous, is possessed of medicinal qualities.

At present we know of only two varieties of the Iris. *Iris versicolor*, and a tall slender variety with paler blue flowers and rounder scapes. The former is the handsomer flower, being beautifully varied with lighter and darker shades of blue, purple and yellow—the latter shade being at the base of the flower leaves. These are again veined with delicate lines and veinings of darker purple.

The name IRIS, as applied to this genus, was bestowed upon it by the ancient Greeks, ever remarkable for their appreciation of the beautiful, on account of the rainbow tinted hues displayed in the

1. LILIUM PHILADELPHICUM.   2. CAMPANULA ROTUNDIFOLIA.   3. CYPRIPEDIUM SPECTABILE.
(Wild orange Red lily.)   (Harebell.)   (Showy Lady's Slipper.)

flowers of many of the species; especially are the prismatic colours shown in the flowers of the large pearly white garden Iris, a plant of Eastern origin, and also in the Persian or Susian Iris.

The Fleur-de-lis, as it was formerly written, signified whiteness or purity. This was changed to Fleur-de-luce, a corruption of Fleur-de-Louis. The blossoms of the plant having been selected by Louis the Seventh of France as his heraldic bearing in the Holy Wars. The flowers of the Iris have ever been favourites with the poet, the architect, and sculptor, as many a fair specimen wrought in stone and marble, or carved in wood, can testify.

The Fleur-de-lis is still the emblem of France.

Longfellow's stanzas to the Iris are very characteristic of that graceful flower:

> Beautiful lily—dwelling by still river,
>   Or solitary mere,
> Or where the sluggish meadow brook delivers
>   Its waters to the weir.
>
> The wind blows, and uplifts thy drooping banner,
>   And around thee throng and run
> The rushes, the green yeomen of thy manor—
>   The outlaws of the sun.
>
> O fleur-de-luce, bloom on, and let the river
>   Linger to kiss thy feet;
> O flower of song, bloom on, and make forever
>   The world more fair and sweet.

Nat. Ord. Ericaceæ.

Small Cranberry.

Vaccínium Oxycóccus.

There's not a flower but shews some touch
In freckle, freck or stain,
Of His unrivalled pencil.
                        Hemans.

THERE is scarcely to be found a lovelier little plant than the common marsh Cranberry. It is of a trailing habit, creeping along the ground, rooting at every joint, and sending up little leafy upright stems, from which spring long slender thready pedicels, each terminated by a delicate peach-blossom tinted flower, nodding on the stalk, so as to throw the narrow pointed petals upward. The leaves are small, of a dark myrtle-green, revolute at the edges, whitish beneath, unequally distributed along the stem. The deep crimson smooth oval berries are collected by the squaws and sold at a high price in the fall of the year.

There are extensive tracts of low, sandy, swampy flats in various portions of Canada, covered with a luxuriant growth of low Cranberries. These spots are known as *Cranberry Marshes;* these places are generally overflowed during the spring; many interesting and rare plants are found in these marshes, with mosses and lichens not to be found elsewhere, low evergreens of the heath family, and some rare plants belonging to the Orchidaceous tribes, such as the beautiful Grass-pink, (*Calopògon pulchéllus*) and Calýpso-borealis.

Not only is the fruit of the low Cranberry in great esteem for tarts and preserves, but it is considered to possess valuable medicinal properties, having been long used in cancerous affections as an outward application—the berries in their uncooked state are acid and powerfully astringent.

This fruit is successfully cultivated for market in many parts of the Northern States of America, and is said to repay the cost of culture in a very profitable manner.

So much in request as Cranberries are for household use, it seems strange that no enterprising person has yet undertaken to supply the markets of Canada. In suitable soil the crop could hardly prove a failure, with care and attention to the selection of the plants at a proper season.

The Cranberry forms one of the sub-orders of the heath family (Ericaceæ), nor are its delicate pink-tinted flowers less beautiful than many of the exotic plants of that tribe, which we rear with care and pains in the green-house and conservatory; yet, growing in our midst as it were, few persons that luxuriate in the rich preserve that is made from the ripe fruit, have ever seen the elegant trailing-plant, with its graceful blossoms and myrtle-like foliage.

The botanical name is of Greek origin, from oxus, sour, and coccus, a berry. The plant thrives best in wet sandy soil and low mossy marshes.

Nat. Ord. Liliaceæ.—(Gray.)

Wild Orange Lily.

Lílium Philadélphicum.

"Consider the lilies of the field, how they grow; they toil not, neither do they spin; and yet I say unto you, that Solomon in all his glory was not arrayed like one of these."

THE word Lily is derived from the Celtic, which signifies *li*, whiteness; also from the Greek, *lirion*. Probably the stately Lily of the garden, *Lilium candidum*, was the flower to which the name was first given, from its ivory whiteness and the exquisite polish of its petals. However that may be, the name LILY is ever associated in our minds with grace and purity, and reminds us of the Saviour of men, who spake of the lilies of the field, how they grew and flourished beneath the care of Him who clothed them in robes of beauty more gorgeous than the kingly garments of Royal Solomon.

Sir James Smith, one of the most celebrated of English botanists, suggests that the lilies alluded to by our Lord may have been *Amaryllis Lutea*, or the Golden Lily of Palestine—the bright yellow blossoms of a plant which abounds in the fields of Judea, and at that moment probably caught his eye; their glowing colour aptly illustrating the subject on which he was about to speak.

The Lily has a wide geographical range, and may be found in some form in every clime.

There are Lilies that bloom within the cold influence of the frigid zone, as well as the more brilliant species that glow beneath the blazing suns of the equator in Africa and Southern Asia.

Dr. Richardson mentions, in his list of Arctic plants, *Lilium Philadélphicum*, our own gorgeous orange (or rather scarlet-spotted Lily.) He remarks that it is called by the Esquimaux "MOUSE-ROOT," from the fact that it is much sought after by the field mice, which feed upon the root. The porcupine also digs for it in the sandy soil in which it delights to grow.

In Kamtschatka the *Lillium pomponium* is used by the natives as an article of food; and in Muscovy the white Narcissus is roasted as a substitute for bread.

The healing qualities of the large white Lily roots and leaves are well known, applied in the form of a poultice to sores and boils. Thus are beauty and usefulness united in this most attractive plant.

The subject of our artist's pencil, the ORANGE LILY, is widely spread over this portion of the American continent, as well as in the more sunny Western States of North America.

We find it, however, more frequently growing on open plain-lands, where the soil is sandy loam. In partially shaded grassy thickets in oak-openings, in the months of June and July, it may be seen mixed with the azure blue Lupine (*Lupine perénnis*), the golden flowered Moccasin (*Cypripèdium pubèscens, Pyrola rotundifòlia,*) the large sweet-scented Wintergreen, and other charming summer flowers. Among these our gay and gorgeous Lily stands conspicuous.

The stem is from 18′ to 2° high. The leaves are narrow-pointed; of a dark green colour, growing in whorls at intervals round the stem. The flowers are from 1–3; large open bells, of a rich orange-scarlet within, spotted with purplish-brown or black. The outer surface of the petals is pale orange; anthers six, on long filaments; pollen of a brick red, or brown colour; stigma three cleft. The Lily belongs to the artificial class and order, *Hexandria monogynia.*

Many flowers increase in beauty of colour and size under cultivation in our gardens, but our glorious Lily can hardly be seen to greater advantage than when growing wild on the open plains and prairies, under the bright skies of its native wilderness.

Nat. Ord. Campánuláceæ.

Canadian Harebell.

Campánula Rotundifòlia.

> "With drooping bells of purest blue
> Thou didst attract my childish view,
> Almost resembling
> The azure butterflies that flew
> Where 'mid the heath thy blossoms grew,
> So lightly trembling."

THE same charming writer has also called the Harebell "the Flower of Memory," and truly the sight of these fair flowers, when found in lonely spots in Canada, has carried one back in thought to the wild heathery moors or sylvan lanes of the mother country.

> "I think upon the heathery hills
> I ae hae lo'ed sae dearly;
> I think upon the wimpling burn
> That wandered by sae clearly."

But sylvan wooded lanes, and heathery moorlands are not characters of our Canadian scenery, and if we would seek the Harebell, we shall find it on the dry gravelly banks of lakes or rivers, or rocky islets, for these are its native haunts.

2. PENSTEMON PUBESCENS.
(Penstemon Beard Tongue.)

1. ROSA BLANDA.
(Early wild Rose.)

Although, in colour and shape of the blossom, the Canadian flower resembles the British one, it is more robust in its growth, less fragile—the flower stems being stouter, and the foot-stalk or pedicel stiffer and less pendulous, and yet sufficiently graceful. The root leaves, which are not very conspicuous during its flowering season, are round, heart-shaped. Those of the flower-stem are numerous, narrow and pointed. This pretty flower is variable in colour and foliage. Its general flowering season is July and August.

The corolla is bell-shaped or campánulate; 5 cleft; calyx lobes, awl shaped, persistent on the seed vessel; stamens 5, style 1, stigmas 2; seed vessel several celled and many seeded: in height the plant varies from a few inches to a foot; number of flowers varying from a few to many.

We have but three known species in Canada, Campánula Americàna, "a large handsome species being found in Western Canada;"* and *C. aparinoides*. The rough-leaved Bellflower is found in thickets where the soil is poor but the atmosphere moist; it is of a climbing or rather clinging habit; the weak slender stem, many branched, laying hold of the grasses and low shrubs that surround it for support, which its rough teeth enable it to do very effectually; in habit it resembles the smaller Gàlium, or Lady's bed-straw. The delicate bell-shaped flowers are marked with fine purple lines within, at the base of the white corolla. The leaves of this species are narrow-linear, rough, with minutely-toothed hairs; the flowers are few, and fade very quickly. The name campánula is from campána, a bell.

---

* Professor Hincks.

The Harebell has often formed the theme of our modern poets, as illustrative of grace and lightness. In the Lady of the Lake we have this pretty couplet when describing Ellen:

> "E'en the light Harebell raised its head
> Elastic from her airy tread."

Our Artist has availed herself of the Canadian Harebell to give airy lightness to her group of native flowers.

NAT. ORD. ORCHIDACEÆ.

Showy Lady's Slipper.

Cypripèdium Spectàbile.

(MOCCASIN FLOWER.)

> But ye have lovely leaves, where we
> May see how soon things have
> Their end, tho' ne'er so brave;
> And after they have bloomed awhile,
> Like us, they sink
>   Into the grave.
>
> HERRICK.

AMONG the many rare and beautiful flowers that adorn our native woods and wilds, few, if any, can compare with the lovely plants belonging to the family to which the central flower of our Artist's group belongs. Where all are so worthy of notice it was difficult to make a choice; happily there is no rivalry to contend with in the case of our Artist's preferences.

There are two beautiful varieties of the species, the pink and white, and purple and white Lady's Slipper (Cypripèdium spectábile), better known by the familiar local name of Moccasin-Flower, a name common in this country to all the plants of this family.

Whether we regard these charming flowers for the singularity of their form, the exquisite texture of their tissues, or the delicate blending of their colours, we must acknowledge them to be altogether lovely and worthy of our admiration.

The subject of the figure in our plate is the Pink-flowered Moccasin; it is chiefly to be found in damp ground, in tamarack swamps, and near forest creeks, where, in groups of several stems, it appears, showing its pure blossoms among the rank and coarser herbage. The stem rises to the height of from 18′ 2° high. The leaves, which are large, ovate, many nerved and plaited, sheathing at the base, clothe the fleshy stem, which terminates in a single sharp-pointed bract above the flower. The flowers are terminal, from one to three, rarely more; though in the large purple and white Lady's Slipper, the older and stronger plants will occasionally throw out three or four blossoms. This variety is found on the dry plain-lands, in grassy thickets, among the oak openings above Rice Lake, and eastward on the hills above the River Trent. This is most likely the plant described by Gray; the soil alone being different. The unfolded buds of this species are most beautiful, having the appearance of slightly flattened globes of delicately-tinted primrose coloured rice-paper.

The large sac-like inflated lip of our Moccasin flower is slightly depressed in front, tinged with rosy pink and striped. The pale thin petals and sepals, two of each, are whitish at first, but turn brown when the flower is more advanced toward maturity. The sepals may be distinguished from the petals; the former being longer than the latter, and by being united at the back of the flower. The column on which the stamens are placed is three-lobed; the two anthers are placed one on either side, under the two lobes; the central lobe is sterile, thick, fleshy, and bent down—in our species it is somewhat blunt and heart-shaped. The stigma is obscurely three-lobed. The root of the Lady's Slipper is a bundle of white fleshy fibres.

One of the remarkable characteristics of the flowers of this genus, and of many of the natural order to which it belongs, is the singular arrangement of the organs of the blossom to the face of some animal or insect. Thus the face of an Indian hound may be seen in the Golden-flowered *Cypèripdium pubéscens;* that of a sheep or ram, with the horns and ears, in *C. arietìnum;* while our "SHOWY LADY'S SLIPPER," (*C. spectábile,*) displays the curious face and peering black eyes of the ape.

One of the rarest and, at the same time, the most beautiful of these flowers, is the "STEMLESS LADY'S SLIPPER," (*C. Acaùle,*) a figure of which will appear in our second volume.

It is a matter of wonder and also of regret, that so few persons have taken the trouble to seek out and cultivate the beautiful native plants with which our country abounds, and which would fully reward them for their pains, as ornaments to the garden border, the shrubbery, the rookery, or the green-house. Our orchidaceous plants alone would be regarded by the foreign florist with great interest.

A time will come when these rare productions of our soil will disappear from among us, and can be found only on those waste and desolate places where the foot of civilized man can hardly penetrate; where the flowers of the wilderness flourish, bloom and decay unseen but by the all-seeing eye of Him who adorns the lonely places of the earth, filling them with beauty and fragrance.

For whom are these solitary objects of beauty reserved? Shall we say with Milton:—

> "Thousands of unseen beings walk this earth,
> Both while we wake and while we sleep:—
> And think though man were none,—
> That earth would want spectators—God want praise."

NAT. ORD. ROSACEÆ.

Early Wild Rose.

Ròsa Blánda.

> "Nor did I wonder at the lilies white,
> Nor praise the deep vermillion of the rose."
> SHAKESPEARE.

> "The rose looks fair, but fairer we it deem,
> For that sweet odour which in it doth live."
> SHAKESPEARE.

OUR Artist has given us in the present plate a charming specimen of one of our native roses. The early flowering Rose (*Ròsa blánda*) is hardly so deeply tinted as our dwarf wild rose, *ròsa lùcida*, but both possess attractions of colour and fragrance; qualities that have made the rose to be the theme of many a poet's song. In the flowery language of the East, beauty and the rose seem almost to be synonymous. The Italian poets are full of allusions to the rose, especially to the red damask rose, which they call "purpurea rosa."

A popular song in the days of Charles the 1st was that beginning with the lines—

> "Gather your roses while you may,
> For time is still a flying,
> And that same flower that blooms to-day,
> To-morrow may be dying."

The leaves of ròsa blánda are pale underneath; leaflets five to seven; flowers blush-pink; stem not very prickly; fruit red and round; the bush from one to three feet in height.

Another of our dwarf wild roses, *R. lùcida*, is widely diffused over Canada; it is found on all open plain-lands, but shuns the deep shade of the forest.

The bark of this wild rose is of a bright red, and the young wood is armed with bristly prickles of a greyish colour. When growing in shade, the half opened flowers and buds are of a deep pink or carmine, but where more exposed in sunny spots, the petals fade to a pale blush-colour. This shrub becomes somewhat troublesome if encouraged in the garden, from the running roots which send up many shoots. In its wild state the dwarf rose seldom exceeds three feet in height; it is the second and older wood that bears the flowers; the flower bearing branches become almost smooth or only remotely thorny. The leaflets vary in number from five to nine; they are sharply serrated at the edges, and smooth on the surface; the globular scarlet fruit is flattened at the eye; of a pleasant sub-acid taste.

This beautiful red-barked rose grows in great profusion on the huckleberry plains above Rice Lake, clothing large tracts of hill and dale, and scenting the evening air at dew-fall with its delicate fragrance.

There is, or used to be, a delicate pale flowered briar rose, having small foliage and numerous blossoms of a low branching habit growing in the high oak-hills in the township of Rawdon. I have never seen the flowers myself, but have heard the plant described as a rare species. The SWAMP ROSE, *Ròsa Carolìna*, is not uncommon; it is

1. NYMPHAEA ODORATA.
(Sweet-scented Water-Lily.)

2. NUPHAR ADVENA.
(Yellow Pond-Lily.)
(Spatter-dock.)

often seen growing at the margin of lakes and rivers, and at the edges of stony islands; it will climb, by aid of supporting trees, to the height of eight and ten feet. The flowers are of a somewhat purplish tinge of pink. The leaves are whitish underneath; this rose is armed with rather stout prickles below on the old woody stem, but smoother above; the flowers are more clustered than in either of the other species.

The sweet briar is often found growing in waste places, and in thickets near clearings—no doubt the seed has been carried thither by birds.

It is very possible that other varieties of the rose tribe may yet be found native to Canadian soil, but the above named are our only known species at present.

NAT. ORD. SCROPHULARIACEÆ.

Pentstemon Beard-Tongue.

Pentstèmon pubéscens.

"Flowers spring up and die ungathered."

THE wild Pentstèmon is a slender, elegant branching plant, not unlike in outline to the fox-glove. The flowers are delicately shaded from white to pale azure-blue, sometimes varying to deeper blue. The corolla is an inflated slender tube, somewhat flattened on the upper side, with a rigid line passing from the base of the tube to the upper lip. There are also two bearded lines within. The lower lip is three-cleft and slightly projecting beyond the two-lobed upper lip; the stamens are five, but one is sterile and thickly beset with fine white hairs (or bearded). The name is derived from a Greek word signifying *five*. The root leaves are broadly lanceolate and coarsely toothed; the upper or stem-leaves narrower, and nearly clasping the stem. The flowers grow on long branching stalks in a loose panicle.

The plant is perennial, from one to two feet in height; it seems addicted to dry gravelly soil on river banks and dry pastures. The Beard-tongue would be well worthy of cultivation; though less showy than the garden varieties, it is not less beautiful and keeps in bloom a long time, from July to September; it might be mixed with the red flowering plants of the garden to great advantage.

Sweet Scented Water Lily.

Nymphæa Odorata.

"Rocked gently there the beautiful Nymphæa
Pillows her bright head."

CALENDER OF FLOWERS.

POND-LILY is the popular name by which this beautiful aquatic plant is known, nor can we find it in our hearts to reject the name of LILY for this ornament of our lakes. The White Nymphæa might indeed be termed "Queen of the Lakes," for truly she sits in regal pride upon her watery throne, a very queen among flowers.

Very lovely are the Water Lilies of England, but their fair sisters of the New World excel them in size and fragrance.

Many of the tribe to which these plants belong are natives of the torrid zone, but our White Pond-Lily (*Nymphæa odorata,*) and the Yellow (*Nùphar àdvena,*) and *Nuphar Kalmiana* only, are able to support the cold winter of Canada. The depth of the water in which they grow enables them to withstand the cold, the frost rarely penetrating to their roots, which are rough and knotted, and often as thick as a man's wrist; white and fleshy. The root-stock is horizontal, sending down fibrous slender rootlets into the soft mud; the stocks that support the leaves and blossoms are round, of an olive-green, containing open pores filled with air, which cause them to be bouyed up in the water. These air-cells may be distinctly seen by cutting the stems across.

The leaves of the Pond-Lily are of a full-green colour, deeply tinged with red toward the fall of the year, so as to give a blood red tinge to the water; they are of a large size, round kidney shaped, of leathery texture, and highly polished surface; resisting the action of the water as if coated with oil or varnish. Over these beds of water-lilies, hundreds of dragon flies of every colour, blue, green, scarlet, and bronze, may be seen like living gems flirting their pearly tinted wings in all the enjoyment of their newly found existence; possibly enjoying the delicious aroma from the odorous lemon scented flowers over which they sport so gaily.

The flowers of the Pond-Lily grow singly at the summit of the round, smooth, fleshy scape. Who that has ever floated upon one of our calm inland lakes, on a warm July or August day, but has been tempted, at the risk of upsetting the frail birch-bark canoe or shallow skiff, to put forth a hand to snatch one of those matchless ivory cups that rest in spotless purity upon the tranquil water, just rising and falling with the movement of the stream; or have gazed with wishful and admiring eyes into the still clear water, at the exquisite buds and half unfolded blossoms that are springing upwards to the air and sun-light.

The hollow boat-shaped sepals of the calyx are four in number, of a bright olive green, smooth and oily in texture. The flowers do not expand fully until they reach the surface. The petals are numerous, hollow (or concave), blunt, of a pure ivory white; very fragrant, having the rich odour of freshly cut lemons; they are set round the surface of the ovary (or seed-vessel) in regular rows, one above the other, gradually lessening in size, till they change by imperceptible gradation into the narrow fleshy petal-like lemon tinted anthers. The pistil is without style, the stigma forming a flat rayed top to the ovary, as in the poppy and many other plants.

On the approach of night our lovely water-nymph gradually closes her petals, and slowly retires to rest within her watery bed, to rise on the following day, to court the warmth and light so necessary for the perfection of the embryo seed; and this continues till the fertilization of the germ has been completed, when the petals shrink and wither, and the seed-vessel sinks down to ripen the fruit in its secret chambers. Thus silently and mysteriously does nature perform her wonderful work, "sought out only by those who have pleasure therein."*

The roots of the Pond Lily contain a large quantity of fecula (flour), which, after repeated washings, may be used for food; they are also made use of in medicine, being cooling and softening; the fresh leaves are used as good dressing for blisters.

The Lotus of Egypt belongs to this family, and not only furnishes magnificent ornaments with which to crown the heads of

---

* In that singular plant, the Eel or Tapegrass, a plant indigenous to our slow flowing waters, the elastic flower bearing stem uncoils to reach the surface of the water, drawn thither by some mysterious hidden attraction towards the pollen bearing flowers, which are produced at the bottom of the water on very short scapes, and which united by the same vegetable instinct break away from the confining bonds that hold them and rise to the surface, where they expand and scatter their fertilizing dust upon the fruit bearing flowers which float around them; these, after a while, coil up again and draw the pod-like ovary down to the bottom of the water, there to ripen and perfect the fruit; a curious fact vouched for by Gray and many other creditable botanists.

their gods and kings, but the seeds also served as food to the people in times of scarcity. The Sacred Lotus (*Nelúmbium speciosum*) was an object itself of religious veneration to the ancient Egyptians.

The Chinese, in some places of that over-populated country, grow the Water Lilies upon their lakes for the sake of the nourishment yielded by the roots and seeds.

"Lotus-eaters," says that valuable writer on the Medical Botany of America, Dr. Charles Lee, "not only abound in Egypt, but all over the East." "The large fleshy roots of the *Nelúmbium lùteum*, or great Yellow Water Lily, found in our North American lakes, resembles the Sweet Potato (*Batàtas édulis*), and by some of the natives are esteemed equally agreeable and wholesome," observes the same author, "being used as food by the Indians, as well as some of the Tartar tribes."

As yet little value has been attached to this charming plant the White Pond Lily, because its uses have been unknown. It is one of the privileges of the botanist and naturalist to lay open the vegetable treasures that are so lavishly bestowed upon us by the bountiful hand of the Great Creator.

Yellow Pond Lily.

Nùphar Ádvena.

(SPATTER DOCK.)

And there the bright Nymphæa loves to lave,
And spreads her golden orbs along the dimpling wave.

THE Yellow Pond Lily is often found growing in extensive beds, mingled with the White, and though it is less graceful in form, there is yet much to admire in its rich orange-coloured flowers, which appear at a little distance like balls of gold floating on the still waters. The large hollow petal-like sepals that surround the flower, are finely clouded with dark red on the outer side, but of a deep yellow orange within, as also are the strap-like petals and stamens: the stigma, or summit of the pistil, is flat, and 12-24 rayed. The leaves are dark-green, scarcely so large as those of the White Lily, floating on long thick fleshy stalks, flattened on the inner side, and rounded without. The botanical name Nùphar is derived, says Gray, from the Arabic word *Neufar*, signifying Pond Lily.

Our Artist has closely followed nature's own arrangements by grouping these beautiful water plants together.

Where there is a deep deposit of mud in the shallows of still waters we frequently find many different species of aquatics growing promiscuously. The tall lance-like leaf and blue-spiked heads of the stately Pontedèria, keeping guard as it were above the graceful Nymphæa, like a gallant knight with lance in rest, ready to defend his queen, and around these the fair and delicate white flowers of the small arrow-head rest their frail heads upon the water, looking as if the slightest breeze that ruffled its surface would send them from their place of rest.

Beyond this aquatic garden lie beds of wild rice [Zizània aquática] with its floating leaves of emerald green, and waving grassy flowers of straw colour and purple—while nearer to the shore the bright rosy tufts of the Water Persicària, with its dark-green leaves and crimson stalks, delight the eyes of the passer-by.

1. SARRACENIA PURPUREA.
(Side-saddle Flower.)
(Pitcher Plant.)
(Huntsman's Cup.)

Pitcher Plant.

(SOLDIER'S DRINKING CUP.)

Sarracènia Purpurea.

EVEN the most casual observer can hardly pass a bed of these most remarkable plants without being struck by their appearance, indeed, from root to flower, it is every way worthy of our notice and admiration.

The Pitcher Plant is by no means one of those flowers found singly and in inaccessible bogs and dense cedar-swamps, as are some of our rare and lovely Orchids. In almost any grassy swamp, at the borders of low lying lakes, and beaver-meadows, often in wet spongy meadows, it may be found forming large beds of luxuriant growth.

When wet with recent showers or glistening with dew-drops, the rich crimson veinings of the broadly scalloped lip of the tubular leaf (which is thickly beset with fine stiff silvery hairs,) retaining the moisture, shine and glisten in the sun-light.

The root is thick, solid, and fibrous. The tubular leaves are of a reddish tinge on the outer and convex side, but of a delicate light-green within. The texture is soft, smooth, and leathery; the base of the leaf, at the root, is narrow and pipe-stem like, expanding into a large hollow receptacle, capable of containing a wine-glass full of liquid; even in dry seasons this cup is rarely found empty. The hollow form of the leaves, and the broad ewer-like lips, have obtained for the plant its local and wide spread-name of "Pitcher Plant," and "Soldier's Drinking Cup." The last name I had from a poor old emigrant pensioner, when he brought me a specimen of the plant from the banks of a half dried up lake, near which he was located: "Many a draft of blessed water have we poor soldiers had when in Egypt out of the leaves of a plant like this, and we used to call them the 'Soldier's Drinking Cup.'"

Most probably the plant that afforded the *blessed water* to the poor thristy soldiers was the *Nepenthè distillariá*, which plant is found in Egypt and other parts of Africa. Perhaps there are but few among the inhabitants of this well-watered country that have as fully appreciated the value of the PITCHER PLANT as did our poor uneducated Irish pensioner, who said that he always thought that God in His goodness had created the plant to give drink to such as were athirst on a hot and toilsome march; and so he looked with gratitude and admiration on its representative in Canada. Many a lesson may we learn from the lips of the poor and the lowly.

Along the inner portion of the leaf there is a wing or flap which adds to its curious appearance: from this section of the leaf has arisen the somewhat inappropriate name of "*Side-Saddle Flower.*" The evident use of this appendage is to contract the inner side of the leaf, and to produce a corresponding rounding of the outer portion, which is thus thrown back, and enables the moisture more readily to fill the cup. Quantities of small flies, beetles, and other insects, enter the pitcher, possibly for shelter, but are unable to effect a return, owing to the reflexed bristly hairs that line the upper part of the tube and lip, and thus find a watery grave in the moisture that fills the hollow below.

The tall stately flower of the Pitcher Plant is not less worthy of our attention than the curiously formed leaves. The smooth round simple scape rises from the centre of the plant to the height of 18′ 2°. The flower is single and terminal, composed of 5 sepals, with three little bracts; 5 blunt broad petals of a dull purplish-red colour, sometimes red and light-yellowish green; and in one variety the petals are mostly of a pale-green hue, and there is an absence of the crimson veins in the leafage. The petals are incurved or bent downwards towards the centre. The stamens are numerous. The ovary is 5-celled, and the style is expanded at the summit into a 5 angled, 5 rayed umbrella-like hood, which conceals beneath it 5 delicate rays, each terminating in a little hooked stigma. The capsule or seed vessel is 5-celled and 5-valved; seeds numerous.

I have been more minute in the description of this interesting plant, because much of its peculiar organziation is hidden from the eye, and cannot be recognized in a drawing, unless a strictly botanical one, with all its interior parts dissected, and because the Pitcher Plant has lately attracted much attention by its reputed medicinal qualities in cases of small-pox, that loathsome scourge of the human race. A decoction from the root of this plant has been said to lessen all the more violent symptoms of the disorder. If this be really so, its use and application should be widely spread; fortunately, the remedy would be in the power of every one; like many of our sanative herbs it is to be found without difficulty, and being so remarkable in its appearance can never be mistaken by the most ignorant of our country herbalists for any injurious substitute.

Note.—The figure represented in our plate, was supposed to be the Pitcher Plant in *flower*, but unfortunately when it was too late to alter it, we found a specimen in blossom. There are five brilliant crimson petals surrounding the umbrella-like hood. The plate shows the plant after they have dropped off. If our book reaches a second edition, this mistake will be rectified.—A. F. G.

NAT. ORD. RANUNCULÀCEÆ.

Liver-Leaf—Wind-Flower.

(SHARP LOBED HEPÁTICA.)

Hepática Acutíloba.

"Lodged in sunny clefts,
  Where the cold breeze come not, blooms alone
  The little Wind-flower, whose just opened eye
  Is blue, as the spring heaven it gazes at."

BRYANT.

THE American poet, Bryant, has many happy allusions to the hepática under the name of "WIND-FLOWER," the more common name among our Canadian settlers, is "SNOW-FLOWER," it being the first blossom that appears directly after the melting off of the winter snows.

In the forest—in open grassy old woods, on banks and upturned roots of trees, this sweet flower gladdens the eye with its cheerful starry blossoms; every child knows it and fills its hands and bosom with its flowers, pink, blue, deep azure and pure white. What the daisy is to England, the Snow-flower or Liver-leaf is to Canada. It lingers long within the forest shade, coyly retreating within its sheltering glades from the open glare of the sun: though for a time it will not refuse to bloom within the garden borders, when transplanted early in spring, and doubtless if properly supplied with black mould from the woods and partially sheltered by shrubs it would continue to grow and flourish with us constantly.

We have two sorts *H. acutiloba*, and *H. triloba*. A large variety has been found on Long Island in Rice Lake; the leaves of which are *five lobed;* the lobes much rounded, the leaf stalks stout, densely silky, the flowers large, of a deep purple blue. This handsome plant throve under careful cultivation and proved highly ornamental.

The small round closely folded buds of the hepática appear before the white silky leaves unfold themselves, though many of the old leaves of the former year remain persistent through the winter. The buds rise from the centre of a silken bed of soft sheaths and young leaves, as if nature kindly provided for the warmth and protection of these early flowers with parental care.

Later in the season, the young leaves expand just before the flowers drop off. The white flowered is the most common among our hepáticas, but varieties may be seen of many hues; waxen-pink, pale blue and azure blue with intermediate shades and tints.

The Hepática belongs to the Nat. Ord. Ranunculàceæ, the crow-foot family, but possesses none of the acrid and poisonous qualities of the Ranunculus proper being used in medicine, as a mild tonic, by the American herb doctors in fevers and disorders of the liver.

It is very probable that its healing virtues in complaints of the liver gave rise to its common name in old times, some assign the name to the form of the lobed leaf.

Bellwort.

(WOOD DAFFODIL.)

Uvulària Grandiflòra.

> "Fair Daffodils we weep to see
>   Thee haste away so soon,
> As yet the early rising sun
>   Has not attained his noon.
> Stay, Stay!—
> Until the hasting day
>   Has run,
>   But to the evening song;
>   When having prayed together we
> Will go with you along."   HERRICK.

THIS slender drooping flower of early spring, is known by the name of BELLWORT, from its pendant lily-like bells; and by some it is better known as the *Wood-Daffodil,* to which its yellow blossoms bear some remote resemblance.

The flowers of the Bellwort are of a pale greenish-yellow; the divisions of the petal-like sepals are six, deeply divided, pointed and slightly twisted or waved, drooping from slender thready pedicels terminating the branches; the stem of the plant is divided into two portions, one of which is barren of flowers. The leaves are of a pale green, smooth, and in the largest species perfoliate, clasping the stem.

The root (or rhizome) is white, fleshy and tuberous. The Bellwort is common in rich shady woods and grassy thickets, and on moist alluvial soil on the banks of streams, where it attains to the height of 18′-20°. It is an elegant, but not very showy flower—remarkable more for its graceful pendant straw-coloured or pale yellow blossoms, than for its brilliancy. It belongs to a sub-order of the Lily Tribe. There are two species in Canada—the large Bellwort—*Uvulària Grandiflòra* and *U. Perfoliàta*—possibly we also possess the third, enumerated by Dr. Gray, *U. Sessilifòlia.*

3. ANEMONE NEMOROSA.
(Wood Anemone.)

2. UVULARIA GRANDIFLORA.
(Large flowered bellwort.)

4. CLAYTONIA VIRGINICA.
(Spring Beauty.)

1. HEPATICA ACUTILOBA.
(Sharp lobed Hepatica.)

NAT. ORD. RANUNCULÀCEÆ.

Wood Anemone.

Anemòne Nemoròsa.

"Within the wood,
  Whose young and half transparent leaves,
  Scarce cast a shade; gay circles of anemònes,
  Danced on their stalks."

BRYANT.

THE Classical name ANEMONE is derived from a Greek word, which signifies the *wind,* because it was thought that the flower opened out its blossoms only when the wind was blowing. Whatever the habits of the Anemòne of the Grecian Isles may be, assuredly in their native haunts in this country, the blossoms open alike in windy weather or in calm; in shade or in sunshine. It is more likely that the wind acting upon the downy seeds of some species and dispersing them abroad, has been the origin of the idea, and has given birth to the popular name which poets have made familiar to the ear with many sweet lines. Bryant, who is the American poet of nature, for he seems to revel in all that is fair among the flowers and streams and rocks and forest shades, has also given the name of "*wind-flower*" to the blue hepática.

The subject of our plate, the little white pink-edged flower at the left hand corner of the group, is *Anemòne Nemoròsa,* the smaller "WOOD ANEMONE."

This pretty delicate species loves the moderate shade of groves and thickets, it is often found in open pinelands of second growth, and evidently prefers a light and somewhat sandy soil to any other; with glimpses of sunshine stealing down upon it.

The Wood Anemòne is from 4′--9′ but seldom taller, the five rounded sepals which form the flower are white, tinged with a purplish-red or dull pink on the outside. The leaves are three parted, divided again in three, toothed and sharply cut and somewhat coarse in texture; the three upper stem leaves form an involucre about midway between the root and the flower-cup.

Our Wood Anemòne is a cheerful little flower gladdening us with its blossoms early in the month of May. It is very abundant in the neighbourhood of Toronto, on the grassy banks and piney-dells at Dover Court, and elsewhere.

> " There thickly strewn in woodland bowers,
> Anemònes their stars unfold."

A somewhat taller species with very white starry flowers, is found on gravelly banks under the shade of shrubs near the small lakes formed by the Otonabee river, *N. Douro*, where also, we find the downy seeded species known as "Thimble-weed" *Anemòne cylindrica* from the cylindrical heads of fruit, the "Thimble-weed" is not very attractive for beauty of colour; the flower is greenish-white, small, two of the sepals being shorter and less conspicuous than the others, the plant is from 1° 2° high the leaves of the cut and pointed involucre are coarse; of a dull green, surrounding the several long flower-stalks. The soft cottony seeds remain in close heads through the winter, till the spring breezes disperse them.

The largest species of our native Anemònes is *A. Virginiàna.* "TALL ANEMONE." This handsome plant loves the shores of lakes and streams; damp rich ground suits it well, as it grows freely in such soil, and under moderate shade when transferred to the garden.

The foliage of the tall Anemòne is coarse, growing in whorls round the stem, divisions of the leaf three parted, sharply pointed and toothed. In this, as in all the species, the coloured sepals, (or calyx leaves) form the flower. The outer surface of the flower is covered with minute silky hairs, the round flattened silky buds rise singly on tall naked stems, the upper series are supplied with two small leaflets embracing the stalk. The central and largest flowers open first, the lateral or outer ones as these fade away; thus a succession of blossoms is produced, which continue to bloom for several weeks. The flowers of this sort, under cultivation, become larger and handsomer than in their wild state, ivory white, tinged with purple. The Anemòne is always a favourite flower wherever it may be seen, whether in British woods, on Alpine heights, or in Canadian wilds; on banks of lonely lakes and forest streams; or in the garden parterre, where it is rivalled by few other flowers in grace of form or splendour of colour.

NAT. ORD. PORTULACACEÆ.

Spring Beauty.

Claytònia Virgínica.

> Where the fire had smoked and smouldered
> Saw the earliest flower of Spring time,
> Saw the beauty of the Spring time,
> Saw the Miskodeed (*) in blossom.
>
> HIAWATHA.

THIS simple, delicate little plant is one of our earliest April flowers. In warm springs it is almost exclusively an April flower, but in cold and backward seasons, it often delays its blossoming time till May.

Partially hidden beneath the shelter of old decaying timbers and fallen boughs, its pretty pink buds peep shyly forth. It is often found in partially cleared beech-woods, and in rich moist meadows.

In Canada, there are two species; one with few flowers, white, both leaves and flowers larger than the more common form; the blossoms of the latter are more numerous, smaller, and of a pale pink colour, veined with lines of a deeper rose colour, forming a slender raceme; sometimes the little pedicels or flower stalks are bent or twisted to one side, so as to throw the flowers in one direction.

(*) Miskodeed—Indian name for Spring Beauty.

The scape springs from a small deep tuber, bearing a single pair of soft, oily, succulent leaves. In the white flowered species, these leaves are placed about midway up the stem, but in the pink (*C. Virginica*) the leaves lie closer to the ground, and are smaller and of a dark bluish green hue. Our SPRING BEAUTY well deserves its pretty poetical name. It comes in with the Robin, and the song sparrow, the hepática, and the first white violet; it lingers in shady spots, as if unwilling to desert us till more sunny days have wakened up a wealth of brighter blossoms to gladden the eye; yet the first, and the last, are apt to be most prized by us, with flowers, as well as other treasures.

How infinitely wise and merciful are the arrangements of the Great Creator. Let us instance the connection between BEES and FLOWERS. In cold climates the former lie torpid, or nearly so during the long months of Winter, until the genial rays of the sun and light have quickened vegetation into activity, and buds and blossoms open, containing the nutriment necessary for this busy insect tribe.

The BEES seem made for the Blossoms; the BLOSSOMS for the BEES.

On a bright March morning what sound can be more in harmony with the sunshine and blue skies, than the murmuring of the honey-bees, in a border of cloth of gold crocuses? what sight more cheerful to the eye? But I forget. Canada has few of these sunny flowers, and no March days like those that woo the hive bees from their winter dormitories. And April is with us only a name. We have no April month of rainbow suns and showers. We miss the deep blue skies, and silver throne-like clouds that cast their fleeting shadows over the tender springing grass and corn; we have no mossy lanes odorous with blue violets. One of our old poets thus writes:

> "Ye violets that first appear,
> By your pure purple mantles known,
> Like the proud virgins of the year,
> As if the spring were all your own,
> What are ye when the rose is blown."*

We miss the turfy banks, studded with starry daisies, pale primroses and azure blue-bells.

Our May is bright and sunny, more like to the English March; it is indeed a month of promise—a month of many flowers. But too often its fair buds and blossoms are nipped by frost, "and winter, lingering, chills the lap of May."

In the warmth and shelter of the forest, vegetation appears. The black leaf mould so light and rich, quickens the seedlings into rapid growth, and green leaves and opening buds follow soon after the melting of the snows of winter. The starry blossoms of the hepática, blood-root, bellwort, violets, white, yellow and blue, with the delicate cóptis (gold-thread), come forth and are followed by many a lovely flower, increasing with the more genial seasons of May and June.

But our April flowers are but few, comparatively speaking, and so we prize our early violets, hepáticas and Spring Beauty.

---

* Sir Henry Wotton—written in 1651.